Discovering the United States

Oregon

By Mary Shaw

An Imprint of Abdo Publishing
abdobooks.com

abdobooks.com

Published by Abdo Publishing, a division of ABDO, PO Box 398166, Minneapolis, Minnesota 55439. Kids Core™ is a trademark and logo of Abdo Publishing.

Printed in China.
052024
092024

Cover Photo: Kimberly Shavender/Shutterstock Images
Interior Photos: Bettmann/Getty Images, 4–5; Dan Lewis/Shutterstock Images, 6; Brian Lasenby/Shutterstock Images, 7 (top left); Hugh K. Telleria/Shutterstock Images, 7 (top right); Harald Lueder/Shutterstock Images, 7 (bottom left); iStockphoto, 7 (bottom right); Shutterstock Images, 8, 23; George Cole Photo/Shutterstock Images, 10; George Ostertag/Alamy, 12–13; Frank Fichtmueller/Shutterstock Images, 15; Sherri Buri McDonald/The Register-Guard/AP Images, 17; Ric Tapia/Getty Images Sport/Getty Images, 18; Naya Dadara/Shutterstock Images, 20–21; Nadia Yong/Shutterstock Images, 24; Rick Bowmer/AP Images, 26; Red Line Editorial, 28 (top left), 29 (top); Eugene Kalenkovich/Shutterstock Images, 28 (top right); Gestalt Imagery/Shutterstock Images, 28 (bottom); Josemaria Toscano/Shutterstock Images, 29 (bottom)

Editor: Haley Williams
Series Designer: Katharine Hale

Library of Congress Control Number: 2023949367

Publisher's Cataloging-in-Publication Data

Names: Shaw, Mary, author.
Title: Oregon / by Mary Shaw
Description: Minneapolis, Minnesota: Abdo Publishing, 2025 | Series: Discovering the United States | Includes online resources and index.
Identifiers: ISBN 9781098294076 (lib. bdg.) | ISBN 9798384913344 (ebook)
Subjects: LCSH: U.S. states--Juvenile literature. | Oregon--History--Juvenile literature. | Western States (U.S.)--Juvenile literature. | Physical geography--United States--Juvenile literature.
Classification: DDC 973--dc23

All population data taken from:
"Estimates of Population by Sex, Race, and Hispanic Origin: April 1, 2020 to July 1, 2022." *US Census Bureau, Population Division*, June 2023, census.gov.

CONTENTS

The Oregon Trail passed through seven states and covered 2,000 miles (3,219 km) between Missouri and Oregon.

CHAPTER 1

A New Home Out West

It was the fall of 1850. Thousands of people had journeyed west on the Oregon Trail. After four months of travel, the **settlers** made it to Oregon. Oregon City marked the end of the trail. The settlers were ready to start their new lives.

In Baker City, people can still see wheel marks in the ground from the wagons that traveled on the Oregon Trail.

More than 300,000 **immigrants** followed the Oregon Trail during the mid-1800s. Many of them traveled in covered wagons. There were a lot of obstacles on the trail. People had to cross rivers and climb mountains. Many got sick or hurt along the way. But they had gone out west to find new opportunities. The settlers who came to Oregon on the Oregon Trail helped shape the state into what it is today.

Oregon Facts

STATE BIRD

Western meadowlark

STATE TREE

Douglas fir

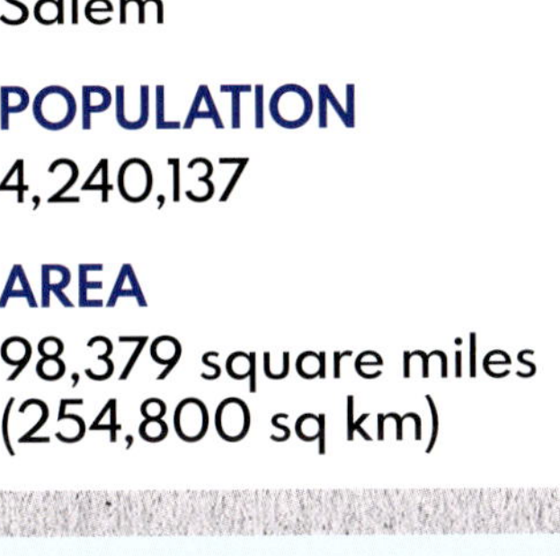

DATE OF STATEHOOD
February 14, 1859

CAPITAL
Salem

POPULATION
4,240,137

AREA
98,379 square miles (254,800 sq km)

STATE FLOWER

Oregon grape

STATE FISH

Chinook salmon

Each US state has a different population, size, and capital city. States also have state symbols.

Oregon's Land

Oregon is in the West region of the United States. The state borders both California and Nevada in the south. Idaho is to the east.

Oregon's flag features 33 stars, which represent Oregon being the thirty-third state to join the United States.

Washington borders Oregon in the north. And the Pacific Ocean is to the west.

Oregon has a varied landscape. **Plateaus**, canyons, and deserts make up the eastern part of the state. Hells Canyon is the deepest canyon in the United States. It is 7,900 feet (2,408 m) deep. Rainforests and beaches run along the western coast. Oregon also has many mountain ranges. The highest point in the state is Mount Hood. It stands 11,239 feet (3,426 m) tall.

Oregon is home to a lot of different wildlife. The American beaver lives in rivers and streams. The western meadowlark lives in the deserts of eastern Oregon.

Haystack Rock

Haystack Rock is one of Oregon's best-known landforms. This large rock sits just off the Oregon coast. Haystack Rock is 235 feet (72 m) tall. It is an important habitat for many creatures. Tufted puffins lay their eggs at the top of the rock. Barnacles and starfish live in tide pools at the bottom.

Oregon's coast is known for being very rocky. Many animals use the rocky landscape for shelter or to raise their young.

Chinook salmon eggs hatch in the Columbia River. Once they become adults, the salmon swim to the Pacific Ocean.

Climate in Oregon

Oregon has many different climates. The climate along the coast is mild and **humid**. It does not get too hot or cold. Western Oregon gets a lot of rain. But there is little to no snow. Farther from the coast, Oregon's climate gets more extreme. Winters are colder, and summers are hotter. Snow falls in the mountains. But eastern Oregon has a drier climate than the west.

Explore Online

Visit the website below. Does it give any new information about Oregon that wasn't in Chapter One?

Oregon

abdocorelibrary.com/discovering-oregon

The Confederated Tribes of Warm Springs is made up of three groups called bands. They are the Wasco, Warm Springs, and Paiute bands.

The People of Oregon

American Indians have lived in what is now Oregon for more than 12,000 years. The Chinook peoples fished for salmon in the Columbia River. Other American Indians also fished and hunted.

Today, many tribal nations continue to call Oregon home.

The state has nine federally recognized tribes. They include the Burns Paiute Tribe and Confederated Tribes of Warm Springs.

French Canadian fur traders lived in Oregon as early as the 1500s. They traded with American Indians. The Oregon Trail brought white settlers to Oregon in the mid- to late 1800s. Throughout the 1870s, many Chinese immigrants came to the state to mine for gold.

In 2022, more than 4.2 million people lived in Oregon. About 74 percent of people were white. Black people made up 2 percent of the population. About 5 percent were Asian, and 2 percent were American Indian. Hispanic or Latino people made up 14 percent of Oregon's population.

Oregon is nicknamed the Beaver State. Fur traders used to hunt beavers in the state and sell the fur to be made into hats.

Culture

Oregon has a variety of dishes. Marionberry pie is a popular dessert. This sweet and tangy blackberry was developed in the state in 1956.

Fresh seafood such as Dungeness crab is common in towns on the coast. Oregon's climate is also perfect for raising dairy cows. The state regularly wins national awards for its cheeses.

Oregon is known for its outdoorsy culture. Many people enjoy fishing, hiking, and skiing. Biking is a popular pastime as well. In major cities, many people use bikes to get around.

Keep Portland Weird

"Keep Portland Weird" is Portland's unofficial **motto**. The city is known for being a little odd. It has costumed bike rides, an insect zoo, hidden tunnels, and more. The city even has its own strange dishes, including fries topped with peanut butter and jelly.

Many hazelnut farms in Oregon are family owned and have been passed down through several generations.

Industry

Oregon has several important industries, including agriculture, lumber, and tourism. Oregon grows 99 percent of US hazelnuts.

Nike is a major sponsor for the sports programs at the University of Oregon.

Many companies in the state create wood and paper products. Tourism provides many people with jobs. Visitors come to Oregon from all over the world to explore its landscapes and cities.

The major sports brands Columbia Sportswear and Nike were **founded** in Oregon. The headquarters for both companies are near Portland. These companies also provide jobs.

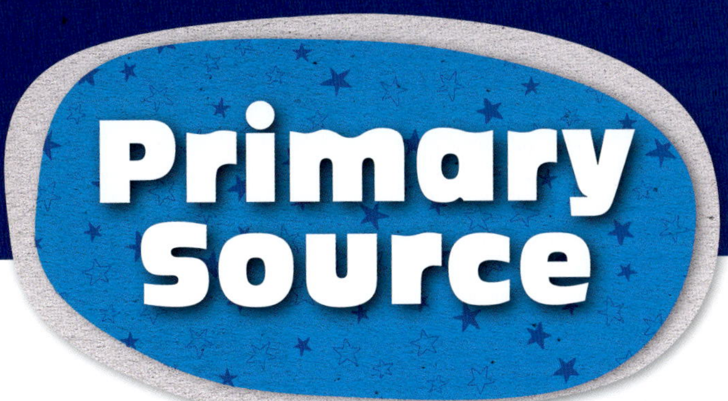

Maria Schur is a Portland biker. She talks about the annual festival in the city known as Pedalpalooza, which brings together people who love biking:

> I love that Pedalpalooza is fun and easy and inclusive. . . . I think it's a great, amazing scene we've created here.

Source: Jonathan Maus. "BikePortland Podcast: Ride Leaders Share Pedalpalooza Memories." *BikePortland*, 27 Sept. 2021, bikeportland.org. Accessed 4 Oct. 2023.

What's the Big Idea?

Read this quote carefully. What is its main idea? Explain how the main idea is supported by details.

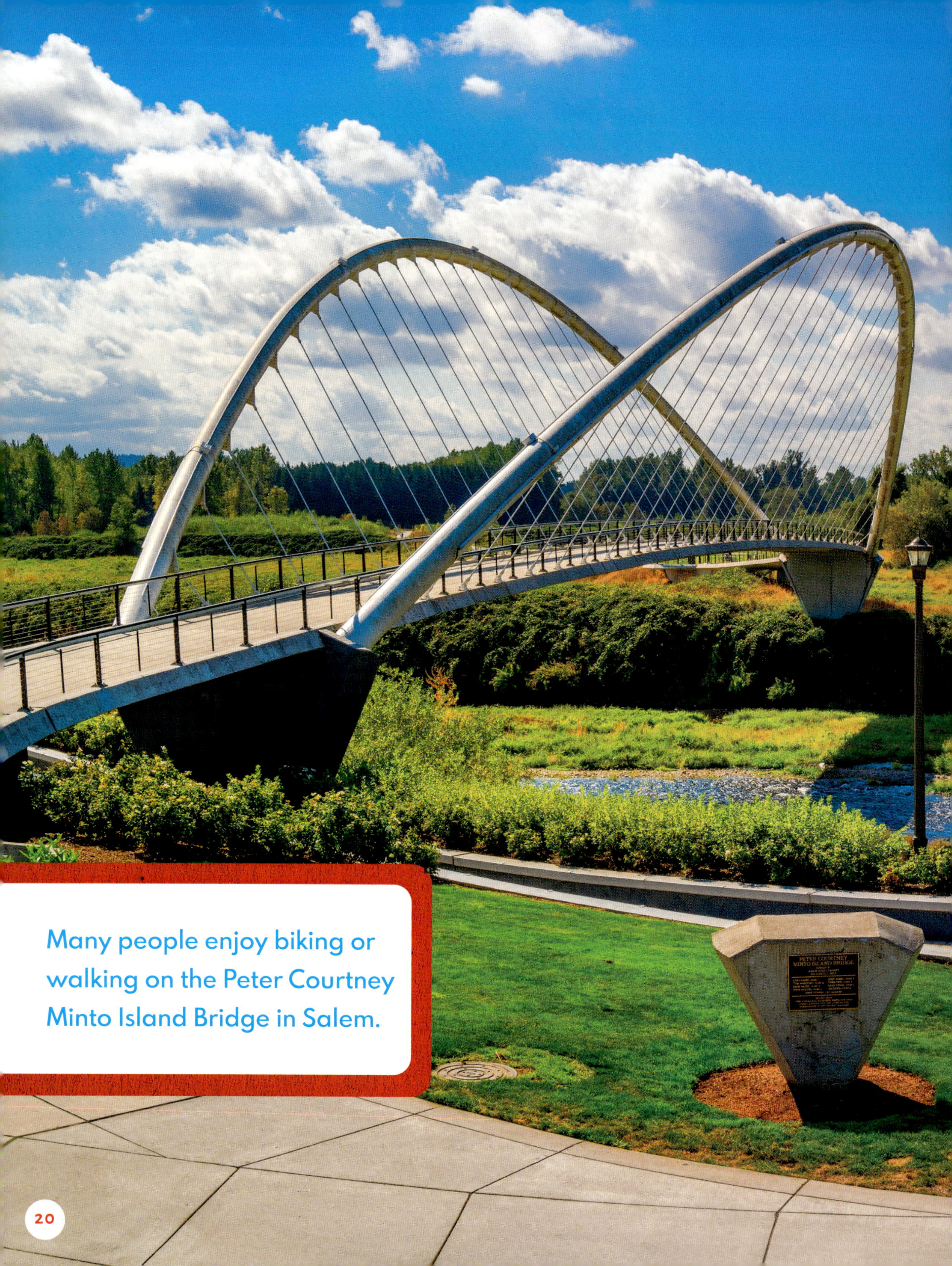

Many people enjoy biking or walking on the Peter Courtney Minto Island Bridge in Salem.

CHAPTER 3

Places in Oregon

The capital of Oregon is Salem. Salem is located along the Willamette River in western Oregon. Portland has the highest population in the state. The city of Eugene is beside the Cascade Mountains. Coos Bay is the most populated coastal town.

There are several American Indian reservations across Oregon. The largest is the Warm Springs Indian Reservation. It stretches from the Cascade Mountains to the Deschutes River.

Parks

Oregon has many national and state parks. Crater Lake National Park has the deepest lake in the United States. It formed when a volcano erupted and left a **caldera**. Over time, the caldera filled with water and became a lake. The water is bright blue and always cold.

There is also an island in the middle of Crater Lake. It is called Wizard Island. Visitors can take

Crater Lake is the deepest lake in the United States at 1,943 feet (592 m) deep.

a boat tour around Wizard Island and learn about its creation.

The John Day Fossil Beds National Monument is another important site. It is in central Oregon.

The Painted Hills are known for their colored stripes. The stripes can be red, black, gold, yellow, orange, or tan.

The monument includes colorful landforms known as the Painted Hills. At Oregon Caves National Monument and Preserve, people can go on guided cave tours.

Landmarks

Oregon has many landmarks. People can visit Mount Hood and go skiing and snowboarding. They can also visit the Timberline Lodge on the mountain. The lodge has been around since 1938. It is a National Historic Landmark. People can stay at the Timberline Lodge and go to one of its many restaurants.

Oregon in the Movies

The 1985 movie *The Goonies* was filmed in Astoria, Oregon. Today, people can visit the house where parts of the movie were filmed. Some movie fans may also recognize the Timberline Lodge. A few scenes from the 1980 horror film *The Shining* were filmed there.

People can go skiing or snowboarding at one of the many ski resorts in Oregon.

Washington Park in Portland has many popular attractions. This includes the Oregon Zoo and the International Rose Test Garden. The garden grows more than 600 kinds of roses. Visitors can see the downtown skyline and Mount Hood from Washington Park.

Oregon has a mix of adventures for everyone. People can hike along the coast or explore underground tunnels in Portland. They can also enjoy local dishes. Whether it's skiing on Mount Hood or biking around the city, Oregon is full of many new experiences.

Further Evidence

Look at the website below. Does it give any new evidence to support Chapter Three?

Crater Lake National Park

abdocorelibrary.com/discovering-oregon

State Map

KEY

Capital

Park

City or town

Point of interest

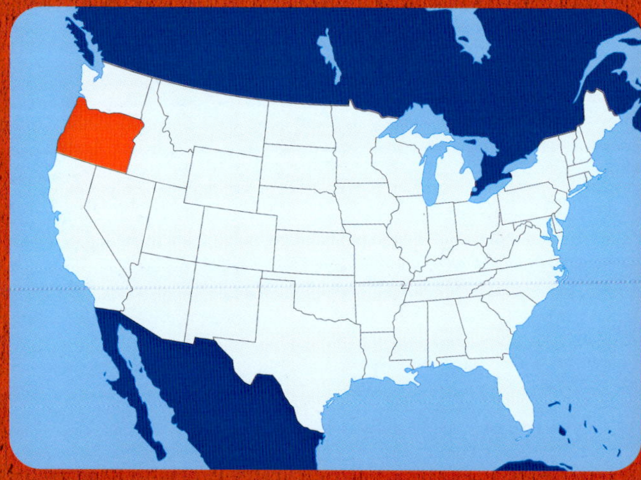

Oregon Caves National Monument

Hells Canyon

Oregon: The Beaver State

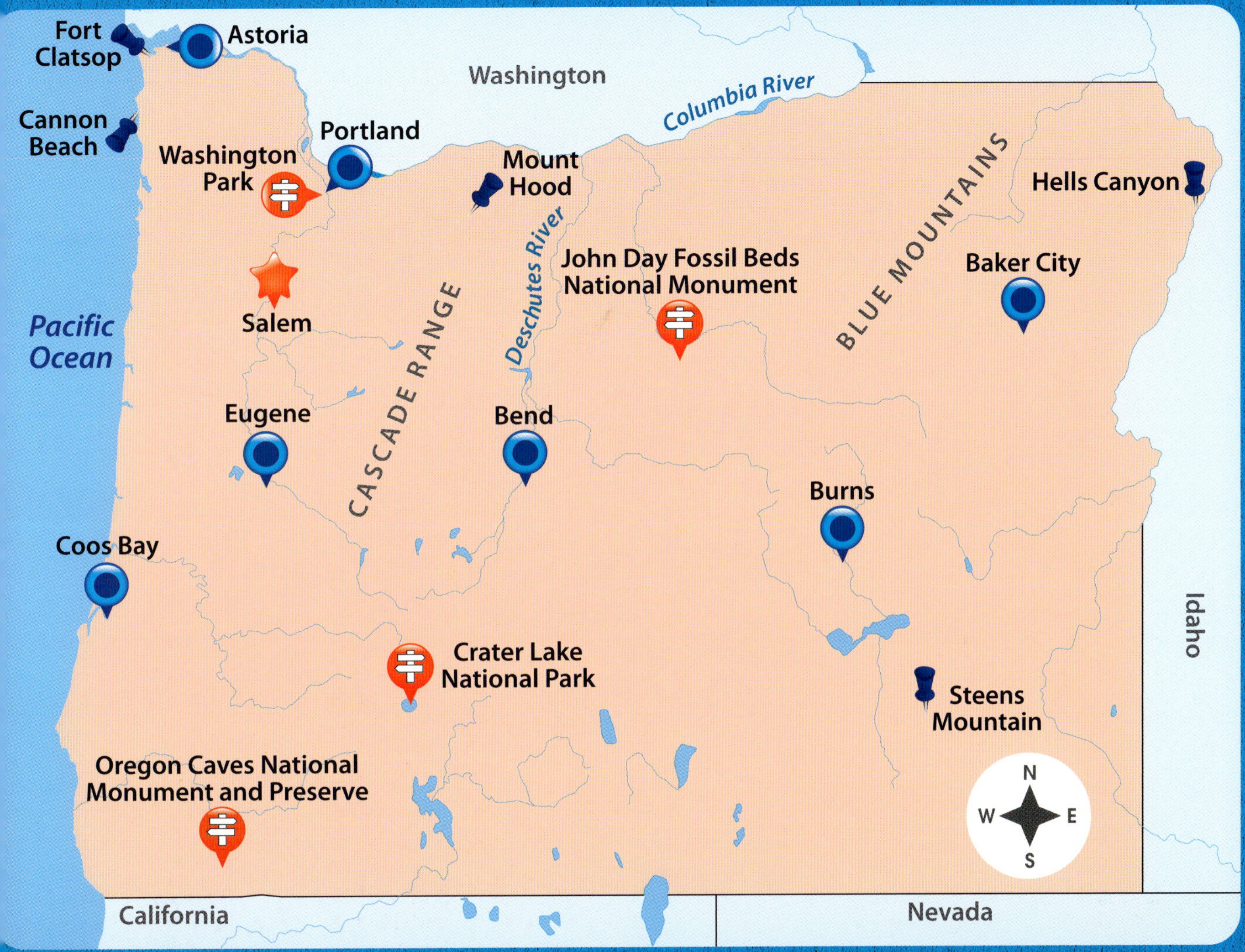

Fort Clatsop
Astoria
Washington
Columbia River
Cannon Beach
Portland
Washington Park
Mount Hood
Salem
Pacific Ocean
CASCADE RANGE
Deschutes River
John Day Fossil Beds National Monument
BLUE MOUNTAINS
Hells Canyon
Baker City
Eugene
Bend
Burns
Coos Bay
Crater Lake National Park
Steens Mountain
Idaho
Oregon Caves National Monument and Preserve
N
W
E
S
California
Nevada

Mount Hood

Glossary

caldera
a hole that forms after a volcano erupts and collapses

founded
set up or created

humid
describing air that has a lot of moisture

immigrants
people who move to a different country

motto
a short sentence or phrase used to describe a belief or the character of something

plateaus
areas of land that are high and flat

settlers
people who moved to a new area

Online Resources

To learn more about Oregon, visit our free resource websites below.

Visit **abdocorelibrary.com** or scan this QR code for free Common Core resources for teachers and students, including vetted activities, multimedia, and booklinks, for deeper subject comprehension.

Visit **abdobooklinks.com** or scan this QR code for free additional online weblinks for further learning. These links are routinely monitored and updated to provide the most current information available.

Learn More

Kavon, Kana. *The 50 States*. DK, 2021.

Tieck, Sarah. *Oregon*. Abdo, 2020.

Walker, Cameron. *National Monuments of the USA*. Wide Eyed Editions, 2023.

Index

About the Author

Mary Shaw writes, edits, and designs children's books. She enjoys visiting family in Oregon and taking hikes on the many beautiful trails that the Beaver State has to offer!